We Are Living

In A Recycling

Of

Humanity

And

Humiliations

GET YOUR SOUL RIGHT
WITH GOD!

By: Theresa Seawood

We Are Living

In A Recycling

Of

Humanity

And

Humiliations

GET YOUR SOUL RIGHT WITH GOD!

By: Theresa Seawood

The purpose of this book....

This work is an inspirational book written

to help others who may be suffering from a

reprobate mind.

My intentions are clear...

"Get your soul right with GOD!"

ACKNOWLEDGEMENTS

I would like to give special thanks and acknowledgements to my family and friends for the encouragement I received while writing this book. Completing this book has been a long journey for me. This book would not be possible without the discernment and presence of God in my life. I also give special thanks to my children Mollie Mae Ellington and Connie Walker. I pray this book be of great inspiration for all those who are struggling with anxiety, depression, broken marriages, relationships, or even those simply seeking God in their lives through Jesus Christ! Last but not least, I dedicate this book to my parents Evans Seawood Sr. and Mollie Mae Seawood, who are both deceased, but may they rest in peace. Thank you Jesus!

TABLE OF CONTENTS

Romans 1: 28-32

28: And even as they did not like to retain God in their knowledge, God gave them over to a reprobate mind, to do things which are not convenient;

29: Being filled with all unrighteousness, fornication, wickedness, covetousness, maliciousness; full of envy, murder, debate, deceit, malignity; whisperers,

30: Backbiters, haters of God, despiteful, proud, boasters, inventors of evil things, disobedient to parents,

31: Without understanding, covenant breakers, without natural affection implacable, unmerciful.

32: Who knowing the judgment of God, that they which commit such things are worthy of death, not only do the same, but have pleasure in them that do them.

FORWARD

Being smitten with the sorrows of pain from a reprobated mind causes depression; leading to suicides, killings, evil massive destructions all over the world, and the list goes on and on with the devil spreading his wings! The abominations of the land prove the bible is being fulfilled! All the signs are here, even in my dreams. Before I started looking up to Jesus Christ praying for him to save my soul, I tried to avoid falling into the depths of man, but that is inevitable without Jesus in my life. I had begun to blame myself, thinking it was only bad luck for me. Now, I'm reading the bible and trying to get a better understanding. I know that the only bad luck is missing heaven and going to hell!

CHAPTER 1

MY AWAKENING

I remember when I was a young girl. I dreamt of God and Jesus coming. I assumed it to be judgment day because it was plain as daylight. I was down on the Gram Farm walking outside in the green grass. I leaned over the fence to look up at the sky. I like looking at the bright blue sky and watching the birds, but that day the sky opened up and a host of angels were on each side of Jesus. Yes, Jesus was in the middle. The angels wore long white robes. Some angels appeared as babies holding trumpets. Jesus wore a long white robe with a red shawl across his shoulder hanging long in front. Jesus had tan skin, reddish curly hair, and a beard.

The clouds began to float as the angels blew their trumpets. I never saw the angels' faces, nor can I tell the color of the trumpets because the angels blended in and out of the clouds. I saw another man in the sky to the left of Jesus. The other man wore a long bronze colored robe. I recall a rope being tied around his waist with bright, huge, beige wings on his back. He held open a black book in his hands. I don't know if it was the bible or the book of life. I believe the other man was God. He looked different. He had a bald head, golden brown skin, and Asian features. In a flash, Jesus held his arm out and pointed down with his hand casting out big balls of fire down destroying the earth. I woke up. I told my mother about my dream. My mother said, "You need to go to church, and stay prayed up, because God is letting you know he can come at any time."

★★★★★★★★★★
<u>Revelations 22:7</u>

7: Behold I come quickly: blessed is he that keepth the sayings of the prophecy of this book.

I grew up in a home where my mother took me to church on Sundays. My family and I attended Macedonia M. B. Baptist Church. Our church was a small white building that sat atop a hill on the Gram Farm. Our congregation consisted of 200 or more people. Reverend Mitchell of Macedonia could preach so well. I remember being baptized at the age of twelve. Although, I accepted Jesus Christ as my Savior, I drifted away from church over the years.

My backsliding into the flesh occurred for many reasons. I have battled stressful relationships while dealing with domestic violence, and fighting back to defend myself. I struggled with broken marriages trying to deal with the suffering of their drug addictions and alcohol abuse, as well as me chewing tobacco. Not to mention, the financial problems that occurred due to lies and cheating. I once again turned to my bible for peace and understanding. I

was not at fault, but rather a victim.

Leviticus 18: 22-24 holds the instructions for us to follow, and the words are so clear.

22: Thou shalt not lie with mankind, as with womankind: it is abomination.

23: Neither shalt thou lie with any beast to defile thyself therewith: neither shall any woman stand before a beast to lie down thereto: it is confusion.

24: Defile not ye yourselves in any of these things: for in all these the nations are defiled which I cast out before you:

Each time I divorced and remarried, I thought it would be until death we part. Instead, the others were no better than the first. It was like jumping from the pot and into the frying pan! I was humiliated each time trying to make our marriage work while feeling like an abused menial! No matter how bad life felt to me, I always said I have God on my side!

I sought solace by reading Hebrews 13:4. I would shout, "God, please help me in the name of Jesus because I fear a reprobate mind! My mind is so scattered.

Please release me from the oppression of anxiety and depression."

> ### Hebrews 13:4
>
> 4: Marriage is honorable in all, and the bed undefiled: but whoremongers and adulterers God will judge.

Right now, I'm thinking biblical, and that is the reason I'm crying out to my Lord God, Jesus Christ, who will never forsake me as stated in Psalms 77: 1-20! God is coming. Therefore, I must not let anyone or anything come before my Lord God, Jesus

Christ, and I again! I think it is good to look back through self-reflection, and then move forward. Self-reflection allows one to identify weaknesses and strength while defining and building character.

> ### 2 Corinthians 13:5
>
> 5: Examine yourselves, whether ye be in the faith; prove your own selves. Know ye not your own selves, how that Jesus Christ is in you, except ye be

That's what I'm trying to do everyday living in these turbulent times. Another reason I'm thinking biblical and telling my dreams is because; I believe we are living in a recycling of humanity and humiliations. Every day and every night it is always something. There is a massive force of destruction all over the world with people killing and slaughtering each other like they are back in the cave men days or the dark ages in an untamed civilization. I pray for the world and a better tomorrow to live in peace and harmony. My life is a good example of living in a recycling of humanity and humiliations. For instance, it was better for me to walk away from the oppressive abuse in my relationships to stop the fighting before we hurt each other

fatally!

CHAPTER 2

PARTNERSHIP WITH GOD

One day while flipping through channels on the television, I came across an Anne Rice interview. Anne Rice said, "Today I quit being a Christian to read my dog ears bible, pray, and serve God." I thought to myself, "Oh! I never read her book, but I can feel where she's coming from." I do not belong to a church, but I do go to different churches seeking an understanding of the word. I try to read the bible, and gain understanding for myself.

Christianity is possible, but requires discipline and will power.

Anne Rice also said in an interview, "I felt like I had been sleeping with the devil." I thought, "That's exactly how I have been feeling, before I decided to become closer to God again." Not only did I feel I was sleeping with the devil, I was eating and living with the devil as well, but prayer changes things. The harder I prayed to God the more I felt stronger with strength and closer to God through faith. God began to reveal my enemies to me through my dreams.

One night, I woke up from a snake pit dream. In the dream, there was a big round bed of snakes squirming among themselves. The snakes were various sizes with some black and some white. I ran through a large grey doubled warehouse door.

Suddenly, a tall black man appeared
out of nowhere wearing a white T-shirt,
blue jeans, and a red cap on his head. The
man was carrying a container filled with

gasoline and poured the fuel over the snakes. With a blasting flame of fire, the snakes started burning, swarming, and crawling on each other. I heard the snakes moaning and groaning. The sounds from the snakes seemed like lost souls all piled up in a bed from hell.

After that, my whole life flashed before me. Parts of my life were good and bad. The devil influences us in many forms or ways with inflictions and affections of both pain and joy to distort the truth behind his actions. This dream symbolized I had an angel protecting me from the snakes. Even through trials and tribulations, God is always with me. I am all wrapped up in grace, and shielded with armor from God. Despite my strength in God, I am humbled. God is my source of strength. Without God, that strength crumbles.

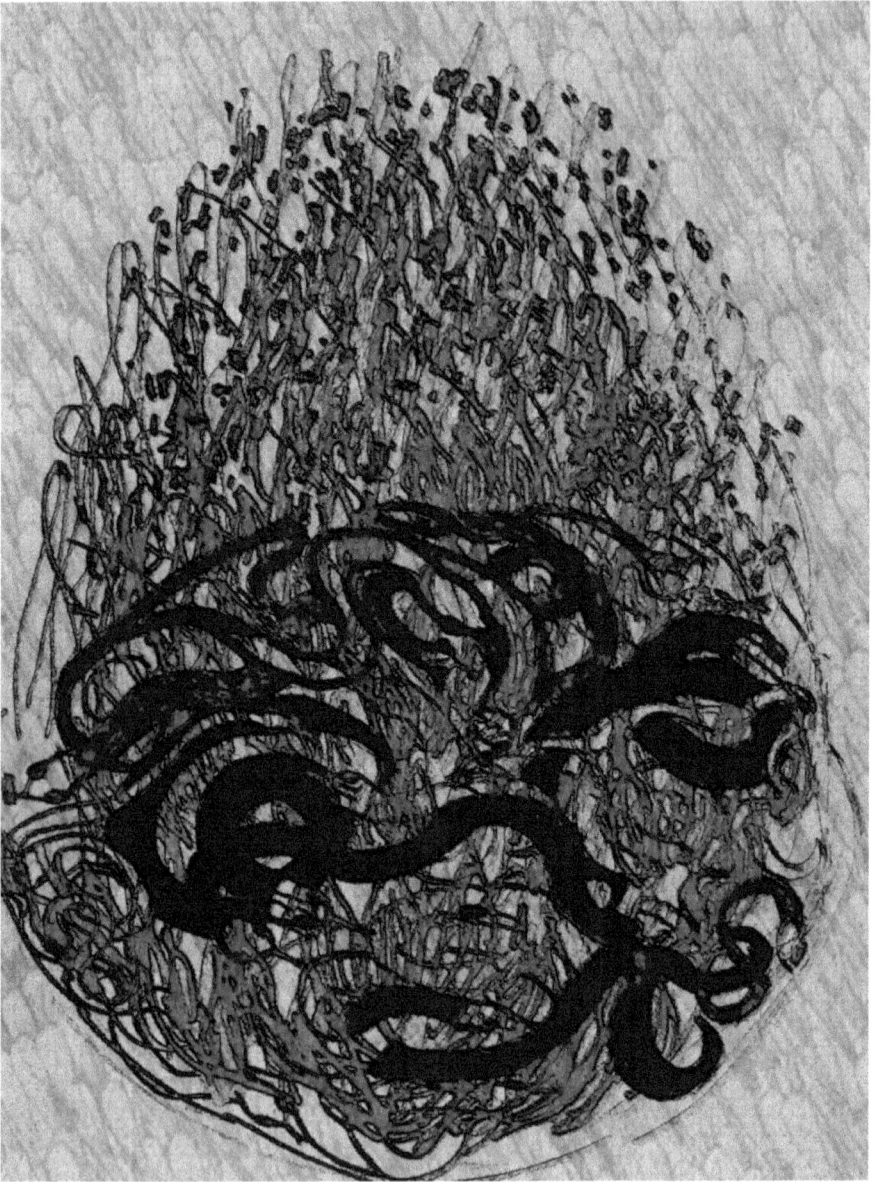

Burning Bed of Snakes!

After my dream about the snakes, my enemies came out of the closest harassing me on my job trying to make me weak and easily broken, because of bad rumors! I stayed to myself and became a loner, and I cried! Especially when reminiscing, my whole life flashes before me when I think of the good times as well as the bad times. My mood goes up and down feeling sad and blue. I'm crying from my deepest soul for help and praying for Jesus to rescue me.

I talked to different people I met when I was out and about as if I met no strangers, just being myself. Some people were friendly and some not so friendly. Deep down inside I feel we all are looking for happiness and try to get it the best way we can! For me being lonely isn't so bad, because after I feel the sadness of sorrows, my life happens. Life happens not only for me, but for the world. I learned to meditate.

As I meditate, I think of goodness and kindness surrounding me to conquer the bad times. In my mind, I am able to pretend the bad times were just dreams. I feel overcome and resolved to keep the faith! I place the good and bad times on a scale in my mind. I have to weigh them out. The good always outweighs the bad. Then, I cry because I'm happy Jesus has lifted me up.

I remain strengthened and humbled, but still naïve at times. For instance, I am reminded of my dream challenging God. I challenged God in my dream by saying, "I won't be afraid to see God face to face." When God appeared before me in my dream, I was afraid to look at him face to face. God pointed his hand at me and said, "You said you wouldn't be afraid to look me in my face." I woke up scared, because even in my dream God let me know...He has the power. I better be ready when he comes, because he is not playing around. Do not challenge God.

God through Jesus Christ is in control of my life! I don't regret following the signs that god has given me to serve Jesus Christ. God demands that we all seek Jesus Christ to eternal life in heaven! I believe my God is my strength through Jesus Christ. I believe that in God's house there is a pure clean, beautiful paradise filled with many mansions.

God is our source of strength, and as stated in Deuteronomy 1:17, we are to have no fear of man. Fear of opposition is unnecessary as stated in 1 Kings 19:1-5. Fear of another's circumstances and the threat of surrounding terror are overcome through the strength of God. For the only One to fear is God. All must have a reverent fear of God as stated in 1 Peter 1:17 and the book of Revelations 11:13. Do not challenge God.

The way I live here on earth, in this world, is only temporary. I believe God sent Jesus Christ to die for my sins. I'm thankful for God's love! When I pray I feel better about myself; because I know Jesus Christ is my true "alter ego." Jesus is a friend I can trust, but my mind is kept whole and protected with God on my side. I pray to keep my connection strong with Jesus because one cannot reach God without Jesus. Prayer gives me great joy and guts to live in this world that is filled with the recycling of humanity and humiliations! Therefore, when God calls me to leave, I hope I have the guts to get

on up out of here. In Jesus name, I pray!

CHAPTER 3

TRUE COLORS

I remember when I was a happy go lucky young woman without a care in the world. I was so naïve and gullible. I would have given my last dollar to someone in need. Yes, my last dollar, but speaking of a dollar, I was looking at the news, and Donald Sterling breaks his silence. Sterling is being sued, because of his racism and racist remarks.

Now, this brings me back with a flashback glimpse to my childhood when the old missionaries use to come around and visit with a bible in their hands to teach the gospel. I will never forget when this old lady said, "The meek shall inherit the earth, and the Ethiopians shall rule the world." Donald Sterling and all the other racists must have missed the message. Well... it's about time Sterling finally releases what has been eating and reprobated his mind all these years.

Satan is surely spreading his wings. I wonder if those missionaries knew what they were talking about back in those days. Did they really have faith? After all, I was a child growing up, but it stuck with me all these years as a reminder of my faith. Today, I visit churches, but I don't hear that message preached. From a biblical standpoint, "Blessed are the meek," as stated in Matthews 5:5.

Racism may even manifest in those who act like your friends until they don't get their way, and then they reveal their true colors. The reprobated individual minds of those who have been hurt create chaos and confusion. It is so humiliating for someone to boast and put another down because they feel superior. For example, I recall when I was about 13; my mother was scorned and humiliated by her boss from the Gram Farm. We lived in a house with only five rooms. Unfortunately, the house burned to the ground, and we all had to move into an even smaller house with three rooms. We were cramped there at that little house for months. Altogether in the house was eight children, plus mom and dad made ten. The three rooms consisted of a kitchen, the front room, and the back room. Back in those days this home was known as a shot gun house or chicken coop. Mom and dad slept in the front room, and the children stayed in the back room. In the back room, I remember some of us having to sleep with two at the head of the bed, and two at the foot.

One day the boss came by looking for my daddy to gather up some field hands. My mom came out on the porch and said, "Mr. Louis, when are you going to have a big house ready for us to move in." Mr. Louis' face turned red, and with a loud outburst replied, "Hell you better be glad I had this one for y'all!" He got in his big blue truck and blew the dust as he drove away. My mom was hurt and said, "We work like slaves, sharecropping, and are treated like dirt." I resented him for treating my mom bad!

My mother told my father what happened when Mr. Louis came over. My daddy said, "We don't have to put up with this much longer because we will be moving into a four bedroom place with a full bathroom and a half bath. We will have a kitchen and a family room. The home is in a low-income housing project." We were all so happy to move. My mother said, "Thank you God for answering my prayers!"

Matthew 7:7

7: Ask, and it shall be given you; seek, and ye shall find; knock, and it shall be opened unto you.

Now that I think about my upbringing on that farm, I realize; Louis Jones acted like it was a privilege for us to be living on his farm working and share cropping with little or no means of support. I say my parents were entitled to the usufruct of his farm! Racism is still present today.

I remember back in 2008, I dreamt Barack Obama coming to visit my family and me, when he was running for president. In the dream, we are in the countryside. A black limousine pulls up to my house. Barack Obama and two men steps out of the car. The men were wearing dark glasses, so I assumed they were his bodyguards. The men stood next to the car while Obama came inside. It seemed like we were kin folks because he sat on the sofa next to me as if he was my brother. Obama smiled saying, "Is there any more ice cream left?" I said, "Yeah, help your-self." Obama gets up and goes into the kitchen. After making a bowl of ice cream, he returned to sit back down on the sofa and began eating. My daughter said, "Mom did you make sure he got a clean spoon," and I said, "Did you?" I woke up telling everyone in my family Barack Obama will be the next President of the United States! I told my neighbor across the street, "Obama will be President."

Now... with all due respect, not trying to be a racist myself, but she is a Caucasian woman, and I am a Black American woman. Despite this neighbor always being so nice, that day she showed her true colors. The neighbor talking ever so calmly with a condescending tone asked me, "Who is he? Where did he come from? Besides he doesn't know enough, or have enough experience, and he can't beat McCain...McCain will be president." The next morning she and a lot of neighbors placed McCain signs in their yards. Even following Barack Obama's victory they kept those signs in their yards for at least three months. All around a lack of respect for the president and a lot of racial slurs. The devil is spreading evil forces, and working all over the world.

One night, I was watching the news, and heard the Korean Central News Agency published an article referring to President Obama as half crossed with unclean blood setting a true example of disrespectful reprobate minds. I have not seen little children behave this bad. Some people in New England town demand the resignation of a police commissioner who admits to calling Obama a racial slur. These are just a few examples of reprobated minded individuals suffering and lacking morals that are disobedient and disrespectful to God.

Colossians 4:4-5

4: That I may make it manifest, as I ought to speak.

5: Walk in wisdom toward them that are without, redeeming the time.

CHAPTER 4

DISOBEDIENCE

Change for the good is hard when our minds are closed to words of wisdom. Open your mind. A simple righteous request goes unheard to those with reprobate minds. For instance, the president has asked males to pull up their pants, but they still walk around with their pants hanging off their buttocks. Sometimes their pants are hanging low showing their underwear or even worse skin. It is disgusting.

Pull Your Pants Up Over Your Buttocks!

If one disobeys God, then I can see why disobeying the President of the United States is so easy to them. God speaks through both good men and women.

Romans 1:28-32

28: And even as they did not like to retain God in their knowledge, God gave them over to a reprobate mind, to do things which are not convenient;

29: Being filled with all unrighteousness, fornication, wickedness, covetousness, maliciousness; full of envy, murder, debate, deceit, malignity; whisperers,

30: Backbiters, haters of God, despiteful, proud, boasters, inventors of evil things, disobedient to parents,

31: Without understanding, covenant breakers, without natural affection implacable, unmerciful.

32: Who knowing the judgment of God, that they which commit such things are worthy of death, not only do the same, but have pleasure in them that do them.

God is giving everybody a chance to repent. Oh, I know it seems so complicated to those who are cursed with reprobate minds, but just read your bible for clarity.

God is showing signs every day, but don't think that the devil is standing still. The devil has so many evil forces going on right now. People please be strong, and cry out to our Lord God and Jesus Christ, because they are the only way to go for help! We are living in a recycling of humanity and humiliations.

Men stop wearing your pants down and grabbing between your legs making gestures of disrespect. Your behavior is projecting the feeling that maybe you have a chip on your shoulders. Look in the mirror and self-reflect, and then you will see the real you. If you keep doing the same thing that brings you no results of good change, you will get what you have always got, which is nothing, but humiliations. I saw a woman ask a man to pull his pants up. The man replied, "I don't bother anybody. I just like to show my ass sometimes when I walk around." For all those who want to show off their asses, go buy yourself a donkey to parade around town.

Judges 5:10

10: Speak, ye that ride on white asses, ye that sit in judgment, and walk by the way.

Disobedience comes in many forms. Terror against mankind in general is the top level of disrespect. In the bible the rules are clear, "Love thy neighbor," one of the Ten Commandments. The terrorist's group Isis is living the life of disobedience.

This group of individuals is an example of those walking around with a reprobated and somnambulistic state of mind. God sends his vengeance to help those who are walking and fighting with faith through Jesus Christ. I believe the group Isis is creating massive terror around the world.

God knows who is wrong, so if it leads to a fight between the United States and Isis, I have faith that the United States will win. The victory for USA is through the mercy and grace of our Lord God and Jesus Christ! Once again, I say, "Wake up

and take a stand for the goodness of Jesus Christ."

Standing In Faith!

CHAPTER 5

REAP WHAT YOU SOW

In one of my dreams, I recall driving in my car. I was accelerating and could not slow down or stop. I was pedaling and pushing at my breaks, but the car continued to accelerate. All around me was darkness. I did not see any houses or lights. I approached the hill, but as I began to descend the hill, I woke up. I did not think anything about the dream until I saw on TV that General Motors is being sued because several people were killed due to a malfunction of the ignition switch in certain models. Now, thousands of GM cars are being recalled. I do feel this is a sign of humiliation to General motors.

I recall the humiliation I experienced working for General Motors when someone hung a hangman's rope on my job. I reported the situation to labor relations, but no one believed me, because my team leader had already taken the rope down when I returned with labor relations. Well, General Motors is hanging themselves with the production of faulty cars, and the people that are suing the company claims the issues are being covered up. The cover-up is another example of the recycling of humanity and humiliation, but one that is close to me personally.

I worked for General Motors for 24 years with only six years to retire as an assembly worker. I performed my jobs very well making sure I made no mistakes. I was the joke of the plant, and remember the snickers and rumors floating in the air. Laughter would fill the air as I approached, and whispers would cloud the atmosphere as I walked pass. After reporting the harassment and abuse I endured from several coworkers to labor relations, my employer released me from my job and management mandated me to see a psychiatrist. If I refused to see a psychiatrist, I was threatened that I would lose my job. Every time I saw my psychiatrist, I was allowed to return to work, but with restrictions. Working did not last as the harassment continued, and I voiced my concerns. My voice always led to another release out on medical. I was afraid during those years and struggled financially. I wondered how I would care for my children. I was depressed trying to return to work.

One day, I called the plant medical office to speak to the plant doctor. The person that answered the phone said, "The doctor's not in, but would you like to leave a message?" I said, "Yes, tell her it's a depression, recession, suppression, so oppress her Ass, and get me back to work!" They let me return to work, but nothing changed. The cycle continued for more than five years from 1997 to 2003. I did not win my case until 2007. General Motors finally released me permanently and retired with 21.5 years. To this day, I still have flashbacks of the humiliations I experienced while working for General Motors.

Psalm 54: 1-7

1: Save me, O God, by thy name, and judge me by the strength.

2: Hear my prayer, O God; give ear to the words of my mouth.

3: For strangers are risen up against me, and oppressors seek after my soul: they have not set God before them. Se'lah.

4: Behold, God is mine helper: the Lord is with them that uphold my soul.

5: He shall reward evil unto mine enemies: cut them off in thy truth.

6: I will freely sacrifice unto thee: I will praise thy name, O Lord; for it is good.

7: For he hath delivered me out of all trouble: and mine eye hath seen his desire

CHAPTER 6
CONFUSED

While watching CNN news, I saw a video tape of Ron Starworth stating, "In 1979, I went undercover as a black member of the KKK for over nine months." Starworth claims he did it so well the KKK considered him one of their most respected members. After a unanimous vote, Starworth claims he was voted leader of the KKK chapter in his area, because of his loyalty and dedication as a Klansman. Now, he has the audacity to wear a T-shirt with the words written on it,

"Inside a black man's mind." To me he is making it seem like he is proud of what he did by saying, "I'm just glad didn't any of the little black girls and boys see burning crosses in their yards." Well, I'm saying, "What about it? Did you make sure the little black girls and boys didn't get lynched?" Starworth's actions are just another example of us living in a recycling of humanity and humiliation. The devil is spreading horrendous hostility throughout the land with his evil forces making it complicated because he wants us in his zone.

I'm still thinking biblical. Starworth's story reminds me of the story of Paul. Before Paul became a loyal teacher of God's word and proclaimer of Jesus' name, Paul persecuted the followers of Jesus. In Act 8:3-8, Jesus blinded Paul, and Paul was given over to a temporary reprobate mind. Paul cried out asking God to forgive him. Starworth don't miss the message.

I recall my father's survival as a child. My father said, "Living in Yazoo, Mississippi was treacherous." My father told stories about how he and his friends would run for their lives from the KKK. My father and his friends saw the KKK lynch men and boys. The KKK would castrate the black men and boys, and throw their private parts in the swamp. So, how did Starworth succeed with going undercover, and he is black? Unless, they made him act out some of their dirty work while wearing white sheets! It is disgusting and humiliating to even admit being there. Now, he wants to give a humane just cause to poetic justice!

□

CHAPTER 7

DEGRADED

One night, I dreamt I was in a truck, and ladybugs were flying and crawling everywhere. So many ladybugs landed on top of my head and body. I jumped out of the truck and started running. I was hitting the ladybugs off of me as I ran away. I woke up, thinking the dream was a sign. Speaking of a sign, I saw on TV in a news break 300 schoolgirls of Nigeria were kidnapped and captured. The kidnapping of those young girls is a recycling of humanity and humiliation. I am praying for myself and those girls. I have to pray for myself because if I don't pray for myself, I won't have the strength to pray for anyone else. I reach out to all of those young girls and pray they return home safe.

Sometime during that week after the capturing of the girls, my sister, and I was in the Hobby Lobby one night shopping with my daughter for her bathroom. Suddenly a speaker announced overhead; the store will be closing in ten minutes. So my daughter rushed to finish some last minute shopping, and time ran out. Another announcement overhead stated, "The store is now closed," and a woman walked over saying, "Its 8 o'clock, please bring your items to the checkout counter, because the store is closed."

After my daughter purchased her items, and we were on our way out of the store, I started talking to the woman, who I assumed to be a store manager. She was the one who unlocked the door, and I said, "I thought I could have sworn Hobby Lobby closed at nine or ten o'clock." The lady replied, "You cannot swear in this store because this is a Christian store." I replied, "I've been praying and trying to save my soul." I started to walk out, but continued speaking and stated, "Speaking of Christianity, don't you think it is bad how people all over the world are fighting, killing, and butchering each other like a slaughter house?" The woman replied, "Yeah, it is." While standing in the door, I told the woman about my ladybugs dream. The woman insisted, "The ladybugs are a good luck sign, but if you ever dream about locust flying, I will know Locusts are a bad sign, call me." We ended the conversation smiling with an "Ok and Goodbye."

The capturing of the school girls is another example of the recycling of humanity humiliation. Some women still feel powerless beneath men. The school girls were punished for attempting to gain knowledge, through education, and for being Christians. The value of the girls was degraded and mocked like slaves in a barter system, a trade-off with an unbalanced equality.

Some women are degraded right here in America! Some are beaten and disrespected in their homes throughout their relationship taking years to leave.

Some never leave. I believe if anyone has God on his or her side through Jesus Christ, one makes better decisions. For example, years ago I worked with a man who thought he could have his way with women. One day he stopped by my job smiling with his hands in his pocket and made a statement, "Body built by Fisher, and mind by Mattel." I said, "Who are you calling a toy?" He said, "You have the body of a woman, but you don't know enough to be a woman!"

At the same time, this adulterer is propositioning me for sex, and shaking a little money that he offered me from his pocket. In return, I told him, "If you even think you are going to touch my cat. I will kill your dog." He quickly responded saying, "I don't have a dog." I said, "See you just admitted you don't have enough to be a man, now take that chump change home to your wife!" I stood strong as a woman, because I had God on my side. I did it through a slick tongue and reversed the insult, but none the less I diverted an ugly situation. Women stay prayed up and seek God for comfort over a man.

Proverbs 8:11

11: For wisdom is better than rubies; and all the things that be desired are not to be compared to it.

Happy and Strong!

CHAPTER 8

DISCERNMENTS

I will never forget the time years ago when I dreamt about tall brick buildings burning and falling down with smoke all around. I woke up to tell my daughter and her friends. I said something is going to happen; I can feel it. A week later I heard about the September 9/11 attack of the Twin Towers in New York. God is getting closer and closer. I woke up thinking... Time is precious.

Something bigger and drastic may happen in the next five years. It seems like some people don't care about what's going on in this world. Some individuals only care about partying and having a good time. Some think only of themselves. If one mentions the Bible some will say, "I don't care about any of that, or it is not doing anything for me." Their behavior is a shame, because we have brave soldiers fighting for our country in this big beautiful world that the Lord God and Jesus Christ are letting us live in.

Mankind, will you please heed the warnings of the time. When one is close to God, a gift of discernment is granted. I know that God gives me signs and discernments. I am not the only one that feels this way. The time is drawing nearer and nearer.

2 Timothy 3:1-7

1: This know also, that in the last days perilous times shall come.

2: For men shall be lovers of their own selves, covetous, boasters, proud, blasphemers, disobedient to parents, unthankful, unholy,

3: Without natural affection, trucebreakers, false accusers, incontinent, fierce, despisers of those that are good,

4: Traitors, heady, high-minded, lovers of pleasures more than lovers of God;

5: Having a form of godliness, but denying the power thereof: from such turn away.

6: For of this sort are they which creep into houses, and lead captive silly women laden with sins, led away with divers lusts,

7: Ever learning, and never able to come to the knowledge of the truth.

I remember driving to my doctor's appointment in January 2014, and my sister was in the car with me. I left early that day, because the news advised there would be winter snow and freezing. While I was driving, I looked at the sky as always for some reason, and that day I said to my sister, "Something is going to happen I can feel it." When I made it to my doctor appointment, she said, "Oh you are early." I replied, "I came early because the news said it would be a freezing storm." I sat down and started talking to my doctor. I told her, "I feel something is going to happen." I said, "One day the sky is going to bust wide open." I started crying saying, "I'm trying to save my soul." I left the office and returned home.

While watching the news another announcement of freezing snow and ice broadcasted. My phone rang. My oldest daughter called stating, "I have to stay over at Grady Hospital to help cover the ice storm." Devastation hit Georgia during the ice storm of 2014. The ice storm trapped teachers and students in a school with no way home, so they remained overnight at the school to wait out the storm. Many individuals spent the night in their cars. God blessed some individuals. A local woman opened the doors of her home to a bus driver stuck in the storm.

The mayor apologized for everything that happened, and said, "I want to make sure the news gets out there quicker the next time and in the future be more prepared." The mayor apologized for the delay and lack of road preparation in some areas of Georgia. Thankfully no deaths occurred as a direct result of the storm, but the storm served as a warning. Get right with God. Natural disasters are not always merciful.

Ironically no one died in the winter storm; however, a plane goes missing in Malaysia with 239 people from flight 370. I remember driving down highway 85 South in Atlanta, GA to purchase a bed from

Under Priced Furniture store. I looked up at the sky and saw a grayish black storm cloud far away in front of me. It was still sunny outside. I saw a streak of airlines in the sky, but no airplane. A sad feeling came over me. I said to myself, "I am going to hear something."

A few days later on the news there was an announcement that flight 370 with 239 people from Malaysia disappeared in the Indian Ocean. Officials are still looking for the plane and the passengers.

The idea of some being caught up and some being left behind is real. During a subsequent visit with my doctor, I shared my thoughts about the disappearance of flight 370. I told my doctor, "Maybe a big whale swallowed the airplane because a whale gets real big, and the ocean is very deep. I cried and said, "Maybe some of the people swam to a remote island and were waiting for someone to rescue them." I pray that out of all those people maybe somebody was saved.

I'm still thinking biblical... Between realities, my dreams, and my faith, I feel a strong discernment and blessing from God. If only one could see and believe in Jesus

Christ as I do, this world would be better. Time is precious. For those of us left here on earth, we must get our souls right with God.

I recall a dream of darkness. In the dream, people are dressed in all black. A crowd of people was running and wandering in the darkness, but one man stood out dressed in a black lace robe. The man started running after me, pointing at me, and shouting, "Where is the gold ring I put on your finger... give me my gold ring, I put on your finger." I woke up and interpreted my dream. The dream symbolized a form of power tripping, guiltiness, and selfishness. I could place the aspect of this dream against many situations in my life including my ex-husband. Some individuals try to make excuses for their behaviors and with animosity request worthless objects back or boast about their efforts.

A real life example, I saw on TV where Donald Sterling boasts about what he has done for the black people while putting Magic Johnson down. Next Magic Johnson said, "I prayed for the man." Now, I'm looking at an 80-year-old man on nationwide TV with tears in his eyes crying wiping his face while talking about getting old and wanting to have a little fun. Well, I'm saying, "How about a little fun with our Lord and Savior Jesus Christ to repent."

Titus 2:1-2

1: But speak thou the things which become sound doctrine:
2: That the aged men be sober, grave, temperate, sound in faith, in charity, in patience.

I also thought of Boko Haram where soldiers are marching around like they are about to renew an untamed civilization. They seem to want to start a revolution with all those captured girls sitting on the ground praying for their lives and waiting for officials to rescue them. I prayed and said, "Help these people in this world Jesus!"

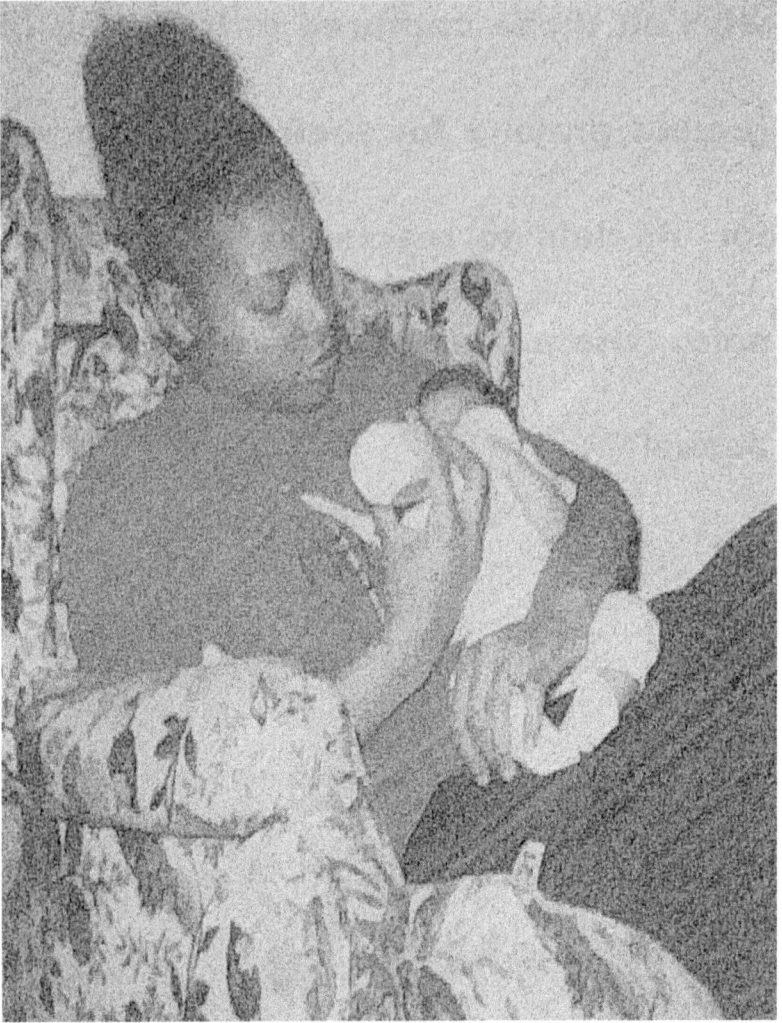

A Strong Caring Mother!

CHAPTER 9

A MOTHER'S LOVE

Confusion and depression are two fatal qualities to mix. I dreamt this summer of 2014 of a newborn baby and in the dream; I pampered the baby with oil and dressed the baby in blue pants and a blue jacket. Now I see on TV, an eight months pregnant Sudanese Christian woman 27 years old is convicted of apostasy or the renunciation of faith! She claims to be a Christian, but the court says she is Islam.

After this mother gave birth to her baby several months passed, and someone released a video on YouTube showing the woman in the jail cell beating her crying baby. The baby is crying for comfort, and the mother is beating and hitting the baby while screaming saying, "Shut up." In the video, one can see a man that appears to be her husband sitting in a wheelchair to the side of her and a small child is present as well. How could her husband let her beat her baby and not stop her? Men step up to be fathers to your children. While waiting for her execution, all of this is occurring. After seeing the video, I paced the floor alone in my apartment, and I cried.

A real mother protects her child and a real grandmother steps in to help. I don't care if they cussed, scream, or even gave them a spanking when needed. I know, because I have lived it. I was proud to push my grandchildren in a cart while shopping, buying groceries, or gifts. I did the best I could to care for them even if I spent my last dollar. Doing so also made my daughter a stronger loving caring mother to her children. The actions against this Christian mother are still an example of the recycling of humanity and humiliations. This mother who is claiming to be a Christian now appears distraught and filled with depression. She appears to be in a temporary state of having a reprobated mind by not showing love to her child. God may have filled her with a strong delusion, but that is between her and God.

In a biblical state, for example, Saul was not permanently reprobated in the context of the scripture for it is defined as those who do not love or retain the truth of God. Refer to the second book of

Thessalonians Chapter 2 verses 10-12 in the bible. In the bible, it clearly states that those who did not receive the love of the truth are given a strong delusion from God. The message is repeated in Romans Chapter 1 verse 24 and 1 Timothy Chapter 4 verse 1.

I'm thinking biblical again and going back when the whole world spoke one language and speech, but the Lord confounds the people's language, so they could not understand one another's speech. God scattered them abroad, because of their disobedience as stated in Genesis Chapter 11 verses 6-9.

Even though we don't speak the same languages anymore, maybe those prosecuting this woman is missing that she is serving the same God like them. Now please, all strong leaders of the world including prophets, preachers, historians, scientists, and all others who are strong-minded to help come together and help us unite! The courts wanted to persecute this young woman like the brutal courts back in the Dark Ages when they burned and killed witches. So they wanted to kill this woman because of her religious beliefs. They humiliated this woman and her family before they finally spared her life. Now, the world can see this is a recycling of humanity and humiliations!

I believe all those who are prejudice and racist are just drowning deep down inside with self-pity and guilty discriminations of who's controlling who. Those prejudice and racist individuals want to be in control, but continuously fail. My prayer is that someday all of the leaders around the world that are truly sent to spread the gospel will come together and congregate with each other to teach everyone about our Lord God and Jesus Christ. When I say this, I speak of the strong leaders who say they are truly born Christians or those sent from God to preach the gospel again!

Matthews 7:14

14: Beware of false prophets, which come to you in sheep's clothing, but inwardly they are ravening wolves.

Make Sure Your Babies Are Happy!

Loving and Caring Grandmother!

CHAPTER 10

NO GREATER SINS

Always remember that no sins are greater than others, because sin is sin, so that's why we have to stay prayed up. It's humiliating when the devil has reeled you under his wings. The only way out is to do some serious soul searching for Jesus Christ! I believe if we don't seek Jesus Christ, God will harden our hearts. Take Pharaoh for instance. My understanding of Pharaoh is that he became too proud sitting on his throne. Having everything a king can have. Pharaoh lacked the obedience to serve and worship God because the devil undermined him into thinking that he could do as he pleases. So, therefore, God harden his heart. For my understanding, Pharaoh is a good example of the recycling of humanity and humiliations. Pharaoh knew who God was. In other words, regardless of the saying, "spare the rod and spoil the child," we as parents still demands that our child obey! Pharaoh did not obey. One can be proud as long as he or she does not let the devil persuade thoughts of thinking that one can do as one pleases. Remember life is not all about self; one must have consideration

for others.

CHAPTER 11

WALK WITH GOD

I am disgusted with the brutal killings that are going on in America. Parents are killing their babies; children are killing their parents, and pedophiles are raping plus murdering children. Oh, it is sickening! Change is needed anytime a young teen runs up inside the school with a knife in each hand stabbing and running amok trying to kill as many people as possible as if he's in danger of his peers. The brutality makes me think what is going on with the school systems? For instance, the act of young teens walking into a school wearing long coats while shooting and killing people like they're in western days. Now it is so sad to me to see and hear on the news that during Memorial Day weekend of 2014 a mass murder was committed by, Elliott Rodgers, who is so twisted in the mind, he blames his unhappiness on the cruelness of women, and hates his pathetic life. So, Rodgers went on a killing spree and murdered six people then committed suicide. He also wounded others and wrote a 141-page story entitled, My Twisted World.

"Oh my," will there ever be a total peace of mind for the mentally ill to keep them from becoming insane and going berserk. I believe their minds have reached beyond a certain dimension or parallel, in Satan's zone. That is why we need God and Jesus in our lives. It seems crazy all over, and you hear about these crimes all over the world as if it's a chess game of crimes. I'm telling the world this is the recycling of humanity and humiliations. The devil will do anything to control the world. The devil wants us to walk around in a somnambulistic state of mind so that he can take over and control us. We all need to wake up and take a stand for the goodness of Jesus Christ!

Anytime sick veterans who have risked their lives for this country are pushed aside like trash in the VA hospitals while being disrespected having to wait months to see a doctor something is wrong. The veterans are not receiving proper care at times proving that we are living in a recycling of humanity and humiliation. People are fighting for their lives all over the world and having someone just come along one day out of nowhere and take lives makes me wonder if the book of revelations is being foreseen.

The crimes are becoming random in pattern; I believe everyone who wants Jesus to save them should stay prayed up including me, because God is nearer than ever! There are people who embrace life and would love to live as long as they could without having a crazed person to come along and take that precious life away!

The VA hospitals are not the only care facilities that are being negligent to patients. There are nursing homes and state hospitals in need of improved quality of care. There are patients with little or no means or resources to help themselves. They become a burden of the state for human resources, which is a better name for the welfare system. I'm giving an example of what happened to my sister Leonia, when I saw her alive for the last time. When I visited her for Labor Day in 2013, I noticed as I was walking toward her, that she was sitting in a wheelchair praying alone. I heard her saying, "Lord I don't want to be here anymore. I'm tired. Please help me Jesus!" My sister looked up at me and our other relatives with an excited, happy look that expressed how happy she was to see us all. I pulled a chair up next to Leonia and gave her a hug. I told her, "I love you," along with the rest of the family. After we talked and asked her how she felt, she yelled out, "They are doping the hell out of me!" We all asked with shock in our tones, "Are they giving you medicine for your health?" Leonia replied, "I am tired of taking the medicine." I remember feeling so sorry for my sister. She could barely walk and could barely feed herself. We stayed at the hotel so we could visit her every day while we were there for three days.

On the last day of our visit, we brought Leonia gifts and we gave her money as an early birthday surprise, because we couldn't be there on her birthday that was September 7th. She was happy for the gifts! Leonia always held on to the bible, and I noticed she had one close by each day we visited. While I was sitting with Leonia, she whispered in my ear and said, "They beat me!" I said, "Who's beating up on you?" Leonia uttered, "The people here beats me" I got up and reported to the staff what Leonia said. A nursing supervisor came over and talked to Leonia asking her questions concerning the matter. Upon examination, the nurse assessed several old scars. The nurse who examined Leonia asked how she got the scars on her body, but Leonia was unable to recall. Some of the scars were from her childhood. When she asked Leonia if someone had been beating her, Leonia said, "I don't know." The nurse claims Leonia mind goes and comes so she may say anything.

After our visit was over we all gave her another hug and said, "We will call you and keep in touch." Suddenly Leonia grabbed at my arm and said, "Take me with you." I said, "Leonia, I sure wish I could, but I can't right now." I walked away with tears in my eyes feeling the pain and sorrow of leaving my sister behind. I was thinking could they be beating my sister and covering it up.

After making it back home, no more than three days later I hear a knock at my door. Without opening the door, I looked at the clock, and said "It's four o'clock in the morning what you want?" My sister Charlean said in a sad voice, "Leonia has passed." I jumped straight up and said, "When?", and my sister responded, "About an hour ago." Leonia passed away on September 6th, one day before her birthday. I feel that my sister is smiling down from heaven! She is in a better place now. Her story is a reminder that more needs to be done to improve the quality of life for patients in long-term care facilities.

I have lost loved one's one too many times. Another sibling of mines, Flora Mae, passed away as well. My dear, older sister

Flora is the benediction and truth for me. I believe in God so powerfully, but so do all my beloved sisters Leonia and Flora. I cried during Leonia's passing, but not only were the tears for Leonia, I have cried for my parents and other siblings as well. Especially in the case of my sister Flora who has touched me deeply! She confessed the pain and suffering she endured before giving her soul to God. A week before my sister Flora passed, I spoke with her over the telephone. Before the conversation, Flora's last words to me were, "It's just me and God", and she hung up the phone!

My sister understood that none of us could help her with her struggle. None of us could take away her pain. Flora held on to her faith even until the end. All of my sisters who have passed were women of God, including my mother. I miss them dearly, but I know that they set strong examples of walking and living in faith. Give the glory to God! □

CHAPTER 12

HE WISHED

I met a dying man back in 2012, which I was friendly with, and he treated me accordingly. He seemed quiet and shy at first, but after we started talking and sharing information about our past it was as if a shell had broken, and out came a friendship that I thought would last a lifetime! This man was wise, and he read me like a book, so he thought. He said to me one day, "You're such a carefree, happy go lucky person, and certain people may misunderstand you for unknown reasons. They will never know the real you until it's too late." With an intrigued look, I asked him, "How do you know?" He said, "My friend let me explain.

I'm living on borrowed times, and I know this just because of the time I have spent with you sharing some of our life stories. I wish I had of met you many years ago. You brightened my day when you came to church and prayed with me. You came to visit me in the hospital, and I could feel your sorrow. You took the time out for me, but I had to see if you were real. I don't have to roll over in my grave to worry about how you're doing. You made this dead man strive to live a little longer! So you go on my friend and be happy go lucky. You will stand the test of times!"

I'll never forget when my dear friend grabbed my hand. He squeezed it with barely any strength while giving me a serious look saying, "If I can recover, I want it to be just you and me. So, if I could get up and out of this bed to take you somewhere, where do you want to go?" With tears in my eyes, I uttered, "We will see. Don't worry." Now, I'm still thinking biblical. I pray for my friend that he is in a better place.

When I see all the dismal prospects of massive destruction and killings all over the world, I sometimes can't help but cry! I also pray for all the people of the world as well as myself, because it is my responsibility. So, as I reach out to this beautiful world our Lord God and Jesus Christ has allowed us to live in, I pray! Even though many prophets have given Him many names, but regardless of his name please keep praying, and if you are misled God will forgive you!

CHAPTER 13

UNITE

My father taught me a long time ago that the Lord God and Jesus Christ will take care of fools and babies. Let us not get so caught up into our idiosyncrasies to the point where we all refuse to come together as people. We must strive for change to live in a peaceful world without war so that our living won't be in vain! As Martin Luther King said, "Brotherhood is the price and condition of survival!"

So, I thought about what John F. Kennedy said afterwards, "Ask not what your country can do for you, but ask what you can do for your country!" I thank the both you, Dr. King and Mr. President, and rest in peace to the both of you. I'm saying the whole world should come together and say, "ask not what we can gain of and from the world; instead we need to come together and repent. After we repent, we must ask our Lord God and Jesus Christ what to do to live in peace and harmony in this world!"

Hebrews 13: 1-3

1: Let brotherly love continue
2: Be not forgetful to entertain strangers to entertain strangers: for thereby some have entertained angels unawares.
3: Remember them that are in bonds, as bound with them; and them which suffer adversity, as being yourselves also in the body.

I'm still thinking biblical. Children are crossing over the borders entering into America to escape from the oppressive abominations and inequities or even the badlands in their country because they believe America is the land of opportunity for a better way of life. Now if we think back when the Lord confound our language and scattered us abroad upon the face of the earth, then living in this time of humanitarian crises should not be a surprise to the world. The crises are enough for any human being to cross over the borders of the land looking for a better way of life!

The grass is not always greener on the other side. After all, a lot of us have heard this land is my land, and this land is your land! On the other hand, once you cross, beware of all the unjust killings by the so-called authorities who are supposed to protect the people and serve justice. I am tired so tired of the young black men in our society being racially profiled. We all deserve to live in peace and happiness in this world if we walk by faith with our Lord God and Jesus Christ. So let us all take a stand and do what is right for the human race. My heart goes out to those targeted by vicious individuals with reprobate minds. Please rest in peace Trayvon Martin and Michael Brown just to name a few.

Also, please rest in peace to all the children of the world whose parents didn't care for them, and only mutilated and murdered them. We are living in a recycling of humanity and humiliations.

Ecclesiastes 5:8-9

8: If thou seest the oppressions of the poor and violent perverting of judgment and justice in a province, marvel not at the matter: for he that is higher than the highest regardeth; and there be higher than they.

9: Moreover the profit of the earth is for all: the king himself is served by the field.

So, after all the killings, beatings, and humiliations, then what do we do? Well, take heed to what Rodney King said, "Why can't we just all get along?" After all, Christopher Columbus discovered America and came from another country. Now that so many children by the thousands are coming for help, some people are upset. Well, if it were your children, wouldn't you want officials to assist and care for your children?

Matthew 25:35
*For I was an **hungred**, and ye gave me meat: I was thirsty, and ye gave me drink: I was a **stranger**, and ye took me in:*

CHAPTER 14

EMPOWERMENT

No one wants to sit in the scorner's seat and be humiliated! Right now this is what the Republicans are doing to President Barack Obama. Republicans are ridiculing and humiliating Obama with threats of impeachment. President Barack Obama is being put down for his great efforts to make goodness in America and throughout the world!

JAMES 1:12

12: Blessed is the man that endureth temptation: for when he is tried, he shall receive the Crown of life, which the lord hath promised to them that love him.

My father and mother taught me that the character in charity begins at home, and then spread it abroad! Men and women who are elected and sworn by oath as leaders of the world, "If you all don't come together as one to resolve your differences worse will happen. Please, unite to help each other throughout the world, to build better agronomics for agriculture, so that people all over the world can work, eat, and live in a safe place, or the crises will continue." Also, keep in mind that God will destroy everything you all have made to hurt each other, because the Lord God and Jesus Christ aren't playing around. Stop belittling our President. Obama says many powerful words to better us as a nation, for instance, he said, "Yes we can!"

When I hear the words yes we can, I think of my father's teachings from my childhood upbringing. My father said there is something on this earth for everyone to do. He said, "Theresa, do what you can, and to do the best you can. Always remember no matter how much education one has to the highest level follow your heart and dreams. Do what makes you feel comfortable, because everybody in this world can't be president, doctors, lawyers, police officers, school teachers, pharmacists, singers, butchers, bus drivers, FBI, directors, detectives, builders, and the list goes on and on. My father said some people are a jack of different trades and at least a master of one while some people can barely do one thing.

Now what my father said makes sense, and this is some of the reasons we are having problems in this world today. A lot of us are trying too hard to do something we are not cut out to be, and some are not trying at all, but only looking for something for nothing. So keep building for a better tomorrow and promise to do your best. So it's not just yes you can or you can't. It's yes you can try, and if it's meant to be it will happen, but it will never happen if you don't try. Get out there and try!

A lot of people have gone to college and passed with good grades, even honor students making the dean's list. Later on these graduates found out that their major did not fit their life goals with respect to the position they wanted to achieve. These individuals did not feel comfortable with the work and felt they were not cut out for it. Some people have never been to college and find work that they are comfortable with knowing they are cut out to do it.

Overall, education is one of the best ways to achieve your goals, but it is not always the only way.

CHAPTER 15

FROM THE BEGINNING TO THE END

My journey in this world is not just about me. I am speaking out to the world to help others through the voice from our Lord God and Jesus Christ. My tears are the tears from Jesus Christ of the world! I have a faith of confessions.

When I sweat, I'm sweating in the blood of Jesus Christ because He died for the sins of the world. It's okay to get up, move, dance, and sweat for Jesus! I don't know when Jesus is coming. As long as it is not too late, one can repent with faith knowing that Jesus is the way to life in heaven. So, therefore, my real address is in my father's house in heaven!

God knows everything from the time our parents conceived us in our Mother's womb, but God still wants us to speak to Him through prayer. God wants us to tell Him what is going on in our lives even though he already knows. The devil can't start anything that the Lord God and Jesus Christ can't finish! All the recycling of humanity and humiliations must come to pass.

Some people believe in first impressions last impressions of people they meet. I don't believe in that myth because people can deceive you. My Lord, God and Jesus Christ will never deceive me. God has let the world know upfront that Jesus Christ is Alpha and Omega, the first and the last to die for all our sins from the beginning to the end! Time is at hand; the whole world is in a code blue condition. Lord God and Jesus Christ will make it a code red when they come marching out of the sky with big fire balls casting down from Jesus Christ hands!

Revelations 20: 12-15

12: And I saw the dead, small and great, stand before God; and the books were opened: and another book was opened, which is the book of life: And the dead were judged out of those things which were written in the books, according to their works.

13: And the sea gave up the dead which were in it; and death and hell delivered up the dead which were in them: and they were judged every man according to their works

14: And death and hell were cast into the lake of fire. This is the second death.

15: And whosoever was not found written in the book of life was cast into the lake of fire.

THE END!

Theresa Seawood

Woman of Wisdom aka WOW!

References

**All Bible Quotations Can Be Found In any KJV
Bible. All thanks to God!**

www.ingramcontent.com/pod-product-compliance
Lightning Source LLC
Chambersburg PA
CBHW061730020426
42331CB00006B/1183